ENGINEERS RULE!

BUILDING AIRCRAFT AND SPACECRAFT

AEROSPACE ENGINEERS

CYNTHIA A. ROBY

PowerKiDS press.

New York

Published in 2016 by The Rosen Publishing Group, Inc.
29 East 21st Street, New York, NY 10010

First Edition

Editor: Caitlin McAneney
Book Design: Katelyn Heinle and Samantha DeMartin

Photo Credits: Cover, p. 5 Monty Rakusen/Cultura/Getty Images; p. 7 (inset) Ineuw/Wikimedia Commons; p. 7 (main) Science Source/Getty Images; p. 9 (Orville and Wilbur) bammesk/Wikimedia Commons; p. 9 (main) Para/Wikimedia Commons; p. 11 Universal History Archive/Universal Images Group/Getty Images; p. 13 (main) Encyclopaedia Britannica/Universal Images Group Editorial/Getty Images; p. 13 (inset) ullstein bild/Getty Images; p. 14 duffman~commonswiki/Wikimedia Commons; p. 15 (Atlantis) Kurun/Wikimedia Commons; p. 15 (Challenger) High Contrast/Wikimedia Commons; p. 15 (Columbia) Clindberg/Wikimedia Commons; p. 15 (Discovery) Craigboy/Wikimedia Commons; p. 15 (Endeavour) Amnerca/Wikimedia Commons; p. 17 Fer Gregory/Shutterstock.com; p. 18 risteski goce/Shutterstock.com; p. 19 (inset) NASA/Getty Images News/Getty Images; p. 19 (main) edobric/Shutterstock.com; p. 21 Colin/Wikimedia Commons; p. 23 (Ochoa) NASA/Hulton Archive/Getty Images; p. 23 (Dyson) VYACHESLAV OSELEDKO/AFP/Getty Images; p. 25 Mark Edward Atkinson/Tracey Lee/Blend Images/Getty Images; pp. 27, 30 Echo/Culture/Getty Images; p. 29 John B. Carnett/Popular Science/Getty Images.

Library of Congress Cataloging-in-Publication Data

Roby, Cynthia, author.
 Building aircraft and spacecraft : aerospace engineers / Cynthia A. Roby.
     pages cm. — (Engineers rule!)
 Includes index.
 ISBN 978-1-5081-4528-8 (pbk.)
 ISBN 978-1-5081-4529-5 (6 pack)
 ISBN 978-1-5081-4530-1 (library binding)
 1. Aerospace engineering—Juvenile literature. 2. Aerospace engineers—Juvenile literature. 3. Rockets (Aeronautics)—Juvenile literature. 4. Space flight—History—Juvenile literature. I. Title. II. Title: Aerospace engineers. III. Series: Engineers rule!
 TL793.R547 2016
 629.1—dc23
                                    2015034087

Manufactured in the United States of America

CPSIA Compliance Information: Batch #BW16PK: For Further Information contact Rosen Publishing, New York, New York at 1-800-237-9932

CONTENTS

FLYING HIGH

People have dreamed of flying for centuries. They've longed to travel to faraway places quickly and explore outer space. Aerospace engineers made these dreams a reality. Today, they're working to help us fly faster and farther than ever before.

Aerospace engineers design, build, and test **vehicles** that fly. They work on aircraft—or vehicles that fly inside Earth's atmosphere—such as airplanes, helicopters, and missiles. They also work on spacecraft—or things that fly in space—such as **satellites**, rockets, and space shuttles. Aerospace engineers who work with aircraft are called aeronautical engineers. Those who work with spacecraft are called astronautical engineers.

Aerospace engineers develop new **technologies** for use in commercial flight, military defense, and space exploration. They design airframes, wings, engines, landing gear, and other devices for these vehicles.

WHERE DO AEROSPACE ENGINEERS WORK?

Aerospace engineers work in many different settings depending on their job. Most aerospace engineers work in office buildings or laboratories. Others work at construction or test sites. Some travel to workplaces both in the United States and overseas. Some design systems that give pilots better control over their aircraft. Others build satellites that help scientists observe **environmental** changes from space. Some work for the military, developing new fighter jets and missiles.

Aerospace engineers have to be creative to come up with new designs. They also have to have a strong background in STEM, which stands for "science, technology, engineering, and math."

FIRSTS IN FLIGHT

People dreamed of flight for centuries before it was possible. In Greek mythology, Icarus and his father, Daedalus, attempted to escape from prison on the Greek island of Crete by flying. Daedalus, a master craftsman, made wings by attaching feathers to wooden frames with wax. However, Icarus flew too close to the sun, the wax melted, and he fell into the sea.

The first human flight took place on June 4, 1783. On that day, French brothers Joseph-Michel and Jacques-Étienne Montgolfier launched a hot-air balloon. They'd discovered that heated air collected inside a bag caused the bag to rise. The brothers filled their balloon with heated air by burning straw and wool beneath the opening at the bottom of the balloon. The balloon rose into the air about 3,000 feet (914.4 m).

The first flights were made with simple technology, but they were huge advances in the field of aerospace engineering.

MONTGOLFIER BALLOON

GIFFARD'S AIRSHIP

THE STEAM-POWERED AIRSHIP

On September 24, 1852, French engineer Henri Giffard's steam-powered airship traveled nearly 17 miles (27.4 km) through Paris, France. The airship was 143 feet (43.6 m) long and was powered by a steam engine, which turned three blades that **propelled** the airship forward. This is considered the first powered flight in history. However, the airship didn't have enough power to fight the high wind that day and return to its starting point.

It would take over a hundred years after the first flight for the airplane to be invented. It took another team of brothers to make a successful airplane a reality.

Orville and Wilbur Wright built and repaired bicycles for a living. They used money from their store to work on their aeronautical inventions and experiments. They used their knowledge of building bicycles using lightweight materials to design and build their plane. They knew it needed lightweight wings, a way to propel it through the air, and means to control it.

On December 17, 1903, Orville made the first controlled, sustained flight in a powered airplane at Kitty Hawk, North Carolina. Named the Wright Flyer, the plane flew 20 feet (6 m) high in the air. The flight lasted 12 seconds and covered 120 feet (36.6 m).

Orville Wright is on the lower wing of the Wright Flyer. Wilbur Wright ran alongside to balance the machine for a controlled takeoff.

ORVILLE WRIGHT

WILBUR WRIGHT

ROCKET SCIENCE

Today, it takes a team of skilled aerospace engineers to design and build rockets to go to space. However, like many early scientific discoveries, the first rocket may have been an accident.

Around 2,000 years ago, the Chinese developed a simple kind of gunpowder. They filled tubes of bamboo with the powder and set them on fire. Some of the tubes would explode, but some would dart out of the fire, powered by the sparks and gases made by the burning powder. These early rockets were used in many Chinese religious festivals. In 1232, the Chinese used rockets to fight invaders from Mongolia.

In the last century, rockets became much more **complex**. In 1969, NASA engineers launched the Saturn V with a crew for the first time on the Apollo 8 mission to the moon.

Thirteen Saturn V rockets were launched from 1967 to 1973. This picture shows the *Apollo 11* space flight.

THE BEGINNING OF ASTRONAUTICS

Discoveries and advancements in flight eventually paved the way for the invention of spacecraft. The ability to build vehicles to explore beyond Earth's atmosphere became a reality in the mid-1900s, thanks to **innovative** aerospace engineers.

On January 31, 1958, the Jupiter C became America's first successful rocket. It launched the first U.S. satellite into orbit. The National Aeronautics and Space Administration (NASA) was founded that same year. On February 20, 1962, NASA launched the first American manned mission to orbit the Earth. John Glenn, an astronaut and engineer, piloted the Mercury *Friendship* 7 spacecraft. *Friendship* 7 traveled extremely fast, reaching speeds of more than 17,000 miles (27,359 km) per hour. The spacecraft made it around Earth three times in only 4 hours and 56 minutes.

John Glenn is shown here, climbing aboard *Friendship* 7 before its launch. A technical issue forced NASA mission controllers to cut the flight short, but Glenn returned to Earth safely.

JUPITER C ROCKET

THE SPACE SHUTTLE ERA

Aerospace engineers, scientists, and technicians teamed up to undertake the huge project of designing and building the first space shuttle. A space shuttle is a vehicle that can be reused for future fights. Space shuttles are built to carry people and cargo to orbiting spacecraft, such as the **International Space Station** (ISS). Engineers designed shuttles to land smoothly back on Earth, which made them reusable for other missions.

NASA's first space shuttle, *Columbia*, launched on April 12, 1981. The *Columbia* was used until 2003. It carried a lab for science experiments called Spacelab. Since then, there have been four other shuttles in use: *Challenger*, *Discovery*, *Atlantis*, and *Endeavour*. These shuttles made 135 space flights altogether. More than 850 people flew on NASA's space shuttles.

This photograph shows the *Discovery* at the end of its mission on October 24, 2000.

ORBITER SKY MILES

Orbiter	First Launch	Distance Flown
Columbia	1981	122.7 million miles (197.5 million km)
Challenger	1983	27.5 million miles (44.3 million km)
Discovery	1984	136.7 million miles (220 million km)
Atlantis	1985	111.3 million miles (179 million km)
Endeavour	1992	115.5 million miles (186 million km)

It took many aerospace engineers to imagine, design, and build the space shuttles. Each part had to be designed and built correctly for the safety of the crew. The materials had to be strong to withstand the conditions in outer space.

The shuttle had three major **components**. The orbiter housed the crew and carried the cargo. Each orbiter was around 120 feet (36.6 m) long. Two rocket boosters helped lift the shuttle in its first minutes in flight. The rocket boosters separated from the shuttle at an altitude of around 24 miles (38.6 km) and then dropped by parachute into the ocean. The exterior tank held fuel that powered the main engines. While the fuel tank burned up after launch, aerospace engineers designed the rocket boosters and orbiter to be reused.

This diagram shows the different components of a space shuttle. The orbiter is the only part that makes it to space.

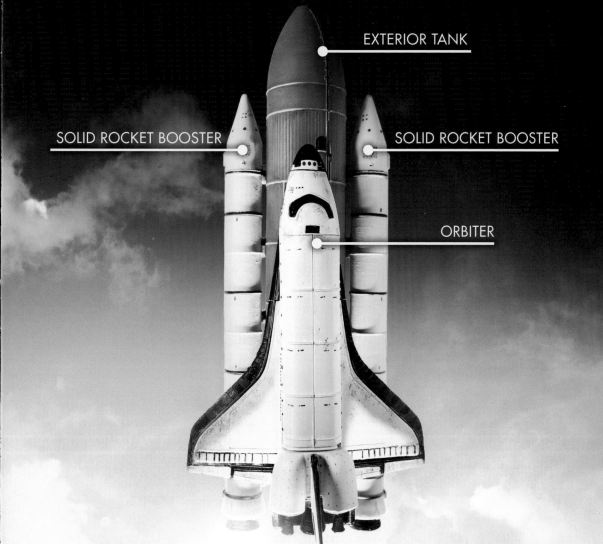

EXTERIOR TANK

SOLID ROCKET BOOSTER

SOLID ROCKET BOOSTER

ORBITER

SPACE PROBES AND DRONES

Because of aerospace engineers, our understanding of faraway and hard-to-reach places has grown.

Aerospace engineers create many unmanned aerial vehicles (or UAVs) to travel to places that are hard to explore in person. These UAVs, also known as drones, can collect information about a place from the

DRONE

air. Drones are used by the military, rescue teams, police, and scientists.

Aerospace engineers also develop space probes, which are unmanned spacecraft. They can travel much farther for a much longer period of time than a spacecraft with a crew. Probes explored the moon in the 1960s. The Mariner 10 probe was launched in 1973, and it flew past Mercury and Venus, collecting important information. In 2011, NASA launched a robotic space rover called Curiosity that would land on Mars. It collects rocks, takes pictures, and studies the conditions there.

NEW HORIZONS SPACE PROBE

New Horizons is a space probe that has flown past Pluto.
It's given us great pictures of the faraway **dwarf planet**.

THE FUTURE OF FLIGHT

What's next for aerospace engineers? Many are hard at work developing better ways to fly faster, safer, and farther. In fact, some engineers are trying to develop mind-controlled flights.

A team of engineers in Germany has developed an **algorithm** that can change brain waves into flight commands. Brain waves have their own patterns, and this algorithm can read the pilots' thoughts about the plane's functions. The technology was tested, and scientists found that pilots were able to do tasks such as taking off and landing just by thinking about the commands.

In order for mind-controlled flight to be used in the real world, however, many more tests need to be done. Aerospace engineers need to be thorough in their tests to make sure flights are always safe for passengers.

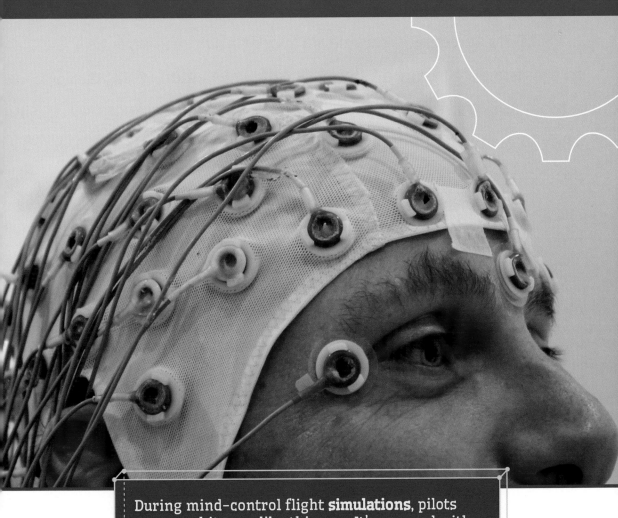

During mind-control flight **simulations**, pilots wear a white cap like this one. It's covered with dozens of **sensors** that record their brain waves.

LEADERS IN THE FIELD

Many aerospace engineers work behind the scenes to create new aircraft and spacecraft. They often work as a team and share the recognition for their achievements. They may not become famous, but aerospace engineers are blazing the path for the future of flight.

Until recent years, engineering was often seen as men's work, but today, many women are leaders in the field. Engineer Anita Sengupta earned her doctorate, the most advanced degree, in aerospace engineering and became the project manager in NASA's Jet Propulsion Laboratory. She helped design a 70-foot (21.3 m) parachute for the Curiosity rover, which helped it reach Mars's surface safely. Elizabeth Bierman is a senior project engineer at Honeywell Aerospace and a past president of the Society of Women Engineers. In 2012, Ellen Ochoa became director of the Johnson Space Center, where many aerospace engineers work.

In 2010, Tracy Caldwell Dyson traveled to the ISS to spend 174 days working as a flight engineer on important expeditions. She performed spacewalks, or walks outside the station, to fix technical problems with the spacecraft.

TRACY CALDWELL DYSON

ELLEN OCHOA

A DAY AT WORK

What does a typical day look like for an aerospace engineer? They may start their day in an office, thinking of new ways to improve a vehicle's design. They may have a specific problem they need to fix with a kind of aircraft, such as a commercial airplane or drone. They meet with other aerospace engineers often to talk about new ideas and figure out the best way to go about a project.

Sometimes, aerospace engineers travel to the places where aircraft and spacecraft are built and fixed. They help workers **install** certain components. Many aerospace engineers work for an engineering company that has customers, or clients. Engineers may meet with their clients to see what they need, whether it's a new navigation system or advanced pilot controls.

A typical day depends what kind of aerospace engineer you are. However, they all have one thing in common—they solve flight-related problems every day.

BECOMING AN AEROSPACE ENGINEER

Do you like problem solving and working on exciting projects? Do you like to figure out how machines work and think of ways to make them better? Are you interested in air and space travel? If so, a career in aerospace engineering might be a great fit for you. How can you become an aerospace engineer?

You can start your career right now by researching more about the history of air and space travel, as well as today's developments in the field. Look at different models of airplanes, spacecraft, and other flight vehicles, and learn about their components.

In school, make sure to pay extra attention in your science and math classes. These classes will help you the most in your career because engineers use these subjects every day.

In high school, make sure to take as many STEM classes as possible. They'll give you a great start in your career.

A career in aerospace engineering usually requires four to seven years of college. A bachelor's degree is the minimum requirement for a starting position. However, most successful aerospace engineers have a master's or doctoral degree. Majoring in engineering, aerospace engineering, or physics will help you learn what you need to know.

Aerospace engineering students learn how to use math and science to design and develop flight vehicles. They study **aerodynamics**, as well as the technology and science behind flight controls, engines, launches, and orbits. Hopeful engineers need to learn everything from the basics of flight technology to the revolutionary technology that's being developed today. They may work at an internship, which is a job where they get paid in experience.

The NASA Academy is a summer project for college students that aims to bring together future leaders interested in space. There are different academies in several locations that focus on space, aeronautics, robotics, and propulsion.

THE SKY IS NEVER THE LIMIT

In the past 50 years, there have been amazing leaps in the field of air and space travel. Each day, there are more than 87,000 flights in the United States alone. Commercial airplanes can carry hundreds of people across continents and oceans to their journey's end. Helicopters can search for people who are in danger. UAVs can explore an area that's hard to reach. And probes, satellites, and space stations can explore what exists beyond Earth.

All these advancements are thanks to aerospace engineers. They've developed the technology necessary to explore our world and the planets and moons of our solar system. In your lifetime, this technology will continue to move forward. No one knows how far we can go! With a career in aerospace engineering, the sky is never the limit.

GLOSSARY

aerodynamics: The science that studies the movement of air and the way objects move through it.

algorithm: A set of steps that are followed in order to solve a mathematical problem or complete a computer process.

complex: Not easy to understand or explain. Also, having to do with something with many parts that work together.

component: A part of something.

dwarf planet: A body in space that orbits the sun and is shaped like a sphere, but is not large enough to disturb other objects from its orbit.

environmental: Having to do with the natural world.

innovative: Using or showing new methods or ideas.

install: To set something up to be used.

International Space Station: A satellite in Earth's orbit launched in 1998 that houses crew members for prolonged periods of time. The station has a research laboratory.

propel: To move something forward.

satellite: An object that circles Earth in order to collect and send information or aid in communication.

sensor: A device that senses heat, light, motion, sound, or smells.

simulation: A representation of the operation of a process by means of another system.

technology: The way people do something using tools and the tools that they use.

vehicle: An object used for carrying or transporting people or goods.

INDEX

WEBSITES

Due to the changing nature of Internet links, PowerKids Press has developed an online list of websites related to the subject of this book. This site is updated regularly. Please use this link to access the list: www.powerkidslinks.com/engin/aero